Leave the Bones

Leave the Bones

Musings of Mind and Spirit

J. MICHAELS

RESOURCE *Publications* · Eugene, Oregon

LEAVE THE BONES
Musings of Mind and Spirit

Resource Publications
An Imprint of Wipf and Stock Publishers
199 W. 8th Ave., Suite 3
Eugene, OR 97401

www.wipfandstock.com

ISBN 13: 978-1-60899-758-9

Manufactured in the U.S.A.

Dedicated to all whom have lost hope
and faith in the material world and seek
a kinder, gentler reality (without all the bones)

Contents

Preface

WHAT SEEMS TO BE obvious is oftentimes misleading. What appears to be trivial may represent a key to magnificence. That which presents itself as reality may, in fact, conceal the truth. Things are not always as they appear, my friends. But is that such a bad thing? Is this orb we call home all that satisfying? Does it take us from birth to fulfillment or just to decay? Shall we truly settle for such a trifle? Will it give us entry and bear us through a better life? Do we get to live forever, without hate, fear, or strife? Do we inherit a permanent home or just a brief pause between dawn and demise? Questions are many, answers are few and unsatisfying. It seems but a pitiful choice, between this and that. But could it be the lie does hide a most remarkable reality? Could it be that we suffer but yet another level of dream? The Buddha declared his wisdom by simply *being awake*. If he has so arisen, shall we but follow suit? All in all, not a bad example, that Jesus and Buddha did produce. Both proclaimed a higher being, both did lend love as clue. Both knew more than ever, about eternal truth. Shall we pay visit to *their* realm of Mind, where angels serenade welcome home souls? Shall we sneak a peek at eternity, just for the helluva of it too? I don't know about you, my friend, but I'm a little bored. I have expended much of my life here, and so far, with little reward. Don't get me wrong. Materially, I've done quite well. It's just that those particular materials haven't served me that well. You know what I'm talking about, that great big hole in our soul. You know of what we are missing; Love and what makes us whole. Deep down inside you know I speak forsooth. Therein does reside the key to our most holy truth. I will help you touch it, if you will allow me. I will assist you in your discovery, if you so trust. But truly, I will show you where I have been. Like or not; an appeal I cannot render true. It simply will be a matter of what rings true to you.

Leave the Bones

Throw me a bone, Joan
A tidbit of false thought
A distraction from truth at best
A direction misguided

More of the senseless patter
More of the loveless way
Keep throwing me those bones, Jones
Meager offerings to tempt me to stay

But as we know, we need more
Than bones to give us life
So seek the fuller feast
Leave the one that is rife
With desolation and scarcity
The one that denies us life

The ego and this world offer nothing
Nothing that we can't do without
Heaven offers everything
We can leave the bones without

Newfound Friend

He doesn't say much
This newfound friend of mine
His thoughts are lightly perceptible
Yet a thoughtful store he minds
He gives me a lot to say
I am honored to carry it on
This newfound friend of mine
Someone called the Son

Tiny Be

In the Holy Instant, for an instant
Fills the cup to overflowing
Brings love to full frontal face
Shows what is worth belonging
Indescribable, though I'll try
If only we may share it
Then brother, you'd be as graced as me
Lighting us both as one
Filled with love, for a tiny be

Silver and Gold

Your silver and gold pale before me
Your illusions, sideshows, and coups
No longer do they attract me
I'm in the act of turning them loose

I've seen a bit of Heaven
I have felt my sweet Father's touch
I have fallen in a sea of love
Never knowing there was so much

I have raised my bar and standard
No longer kneeling to the creed
Eyes set on more splendid places
Places of beauty and peace

So retract your offer, old world
It entices me not
I have no need of trinkets
And trinkets are all you've got

Where I Want To Be

I keep touching that place I see
Elusive though it may be
Love lingers there, I know it
It is where I want to be

A Place Where All Amens

We're off and dancing, my friend
Another small story to be
It's always fun with another
To see what we may see

I adore this collaboration
This union of you and me
I feel like swirling down the hall
As I watch my dancing feat

Years tempted me to sadness
Brought sorrow to my door
Bid me lay down and die
Bury me forever more

I chose the high road instead
I decided to jump on board
Was tired of so much relentless
I needed something more

So I write these tales
And read them with you, my friend
We're off and dancing together
In a procession to timeless end
Our destination is quite holy
A place that never ends
A place where all amens

Going Downtown

I feel like going downtown
To get a slice of life
Seeing the ads and deference
To the world's homely wife

Soon, they'll develop a better
Sleeker look and feel
Something to get me off the dime
And spend it on a lonely meal

Shallow offerings sometimes seem better
Than nothing offered at all
Yet they dry up just as quickly
As the loneliness they forestall

Deeper penetration is needed
Pure waters reside within
To find some means of satisfaction
Than those you've likely been in

No real answers here, my friend
Yet some doozies wait within

Temporary Insanity

We've accepted insanity as sane
And in the process become insane
Willingly accepting the mediocre
Allowing life to carry our bane

Consider for one moment the possibility
That we are in fact quite loony
Ought not we look for the exit
Ought not we do so routinely

If this world be sanity
With all that it portrays
Then leave me alone in the loony bin
I could care less what the normal say

Dare we not expect better
From a God as loving as ours
Dare we not open our eyes
And exchange the world for flowers
Flowers of such profound elegance
That minds are stopped in their tracks
Indiscernible beauty awaits us
We merely need to retract
The chips we hold in this lonely game
And wait for God to call our name

The Key to Heaven

I present you with salvation, my brother
And you, the same for me, as well
We may find Heaven only in each other's company
Walking separately is the way to Hell

So look deep inside, as I have
Find your long held goal
Yet know that it must include me
And every brother within God's Fold

So reach out to me and I to you
In each other we find our wholeness
Where the One replaces the two

We will walk through the Gates of Heaven
Hand in hand, side by side
It is the only way to enter
If in Paradise we intend to abide

It is not enough to be holy
We must do so in collective form
Our Father will only recognize us
When we arrive in a single norm

Let us not hide within any longer
Let us embrace each other in kind
It is the key to Heaven
In each other, this we will find

Tales

Let me choose my label
I know what it should be
I want to be a storyteller
This is right for me
I behold the picture in mind
Of aged storyteller working fine
Weaving tales of wisdom
I know these tales are mine
Not to hold and carry
But to share in His Sweet Name
Stories to enfold us all
Tales with no one to blame

The Pool

Let us all be in love together
Enter the pool of endless depth
Lose ourselves in each other
Join our Blessed Father
The pool contains nothing else

Significant Rhyme

You guys sure know how
To find a man a job
Couldn't have dreamed it better
With the aid of a happy mob

Your wisdom and truth surprised me
I have never been subjected to such
The fineness of your love for me
Unveils the endless much

So thanks for the offer
And the job to end all time
Sharing your wisdom with our brothers
Clothed in significant rhyme

Me and You

Peace opens the door
And joy carries it in
No wonder I feel so well
When the rhyme arrives therein

Give it thought for a moment
And truly you will see
That the words you see before you
Were always meant to be

They waited simply for an offer
To open and let them come through
They've always been waiting for us
To tell us of me and you

Some Kind of Deal

It is clear to me now
That some kind of deal was struck
Something with high appeal
Something that changed my luck

Nicobod and Ichobod led the way
Parted the seas and said, *make way*!
We are the fore of an appointed way
We are the rhyme that comes to stay

Salvation Within the Rhyme

Thank you, J
For our specific way
Though the love extends beyond us
In quite an extraordinary way
This will always be
My favorite adventure of all time
This will always be
Salvation within the rhyme

Faithfully On

I will pass your words, my Brother
Faithfully on, faithfully on
I will devote my life to it
Serving the Holy Son
For our Father has endorsed it
Or else we would not be here
It emanates but from one Source
A place that knows no fear
It is a splendid time, my brother
To lend ear and eye alone
To the truth as it presents you
And the vision of our Home

Holy Day

It's a wonderful day in the Rockies
Snow capped and put on display
Sun arising brings brilliant color
To set upon this day
Beautiful yet smaller
Than I remember them to be
Perhaps it is my perspective
That allows me to finally see
That all here is dwarfed
By Magnificence on display
All here is dissolving
To leave but a holy day

A Poorer Dime

The pain of separation
Is the only pain there is
It resides within our minds
Where it hides the phantom it is

It may manifest in body
It may show in different ways
It may appear as various diseases
Yet it hides its source this way

Find, and heal it, in the mind
Heal it by healing separation
Only then will you find
That fixing a broken illusion
Is akin to splitting a dime
It lessens the value of the effort
While leaving you poorer in time

The Merging of We

Ancient truths in modern clothes
Wearing poems or lovely prose
From whence they come
Our Savior knows

The wise will recognize
The love within the rose
The ready to see will open eyes
And strike a receptive pose

When it is your time, you will know
The words will speak your name
The truth will arrive unexpectedly
You will know we are all the same

If these odes do bless your mind
I am blessed as well, you see
For truth but travels in pairs, my dear
Needed for the merging of we

Enter the Time Machine

Enter the time machine
Leave monuments to time behind
Get set to leave this tardy place
For a whole new place in time
Well actually, that is a misnomer
The machine will *exceed* its time
It will take us to a place suspended
Above all of space and time

Mr. Meek

You expected Mr. Meek
I have no claim to the name
I like to think in humble
And ignore any religious fame

I've got to say, I can't help it
I enjoy a bit of screwing with you
It tweaks my funny bone a bit
And helps us laugh it through

Love flies the wings of laughter
Humor is a loving thing
Pray it delivers kind words to you
Assume sweet smiles it brings

Meek Again

Well, here I am again
It appears we weren't done at all
So I thought to make another
Poem, to carry it all
Mr. Meek is just too interesting
To let him go so soon
I'll need to alter the name somewhat
How about Meek McCrude

Old Meek McCrude

Old Meek McCrude swung a lively pen
The words came out, he put them in
A gunslinger's repertoire of candles
A satchel filled to the brim

Synchronized upon arrival
The letters and sounds attend
Forming up in pearlized words
To display in Meek's coming trends

Old Meek McCrude just walked right in
Sat right down, prepared to begin
An assault on faulty senses
A run at illusory walls
Hoping the words will penetrate
The accumulated but fragile halls
Of false worldly knowledge
Replaced by Heaven's Call

Poems All Day

I love it, my friend
What can I say
I caress my pen in hopes
For another poem this day

Each a blessing within disguise
I'll take them and share them
Let them bless all holy eyes

I love it, my friend
What can I say
I could write these precious odes
All the live long day

Let Me Hear

Let me hear only sweet words
Spoken by Christ in disguise
Let my soul know only light
As seen in my brother's eyes

Let me recognize the Holy Spirit
In each and every sound I hear
Let me hear only silence
Gracing my waiting ear

Let me know by the sound of it
As it leaves my sweet brother's lips
That God is speaking through him
And conveying holy tips

For if I cannot hear my brother
And know his words are Christ's
Then never let me hear again
Until the truth becomes my right

I Am

I cannot see the Christ in me
Until, in my brother, I know Him to be
The rest of me in seeming disguise
Until I see through Christ's holy eyes

The only way to see as one
Is to open my heart to everyone
The only way to know who I am
Is to see and hear and know I Am

Holy Chance

Such wonderful circumstances
Such timely rhythm too
Bringing truth to our doorstep
The truth of me and you

Yet that truth, my friend
Is not really of me and you
For it tells of only one of us
Of the One that shows as two

Salvation waits for only that One
It will never be granted to more
It is our quest and journey
To hear the ancient lore
For in that Book of Ages
Lies truth forever more

That truth is very simply
That we are one and the same
Yet we see with divided eye
That granted of worldly fame

Yet the sight of Christ is in us all
It awaits our awakened glance
No longer will we be seen apart
Let us take this holy chance

Next Door

It's so grand to be going Home
I've been here a long time
Yet always yearning for more
I've been here a very long time
Yet I have read the ancient lore
That points me to the exit
To the Home that lives next door

Masterpiece in Play

Perceptual filters anoint us all
With a lively this/that view
That casts a dim lit pall

Ego cooks it up and serves it
On perspective here and there
Coloring what each will see
Fair or beastly meets our stare

One may say *this is a piece of shit!*
The other may look away
Reaching then back, to say
I disagree on its very nature
It's a masterpiece in play!

My Brother's Voice

I will listen for You, my Captain
In my brother's voice
Knowing You speak but to One of us
Seeing the only choice

I have been deafened by ignorance
Blinded by what I wanted to see
Looking inside for all the answers
When so many came from my brothers to be
Wisdom falling upon deaf ears
Shown to one too blind to see

Now I will look to prayer answered
By way of my brother's heart
Spoken by his words so favored
Demonstrating reunited parts

A Timeslot or Two

In truth, I am but perfect
In the world, I still make mistakes
In my right Mind, I see no error
Yet my ego continues to take
A timeslot or two out of many
Yet I always regret any stay
My quest is to be always perfect
In my True Self, I pray

Dark Cloud

Hate is a cloak not worn well
Tis a darkness upon the soul
Dimming the light hosted within it
Betraying the path foretold

It holds no promise, no truth
Attempting murder on mind and spirit
It darkens the soul who follows
And hosts dire fear within it

It demeans the brother who wears it
It will chew you up inside
Leaving all hopeless who see fit
To accompany its loveless ride
Shed it like the plague it is
Let love cause *it* to hide

Thanking God and Joan Jones

Our story begins with the author
Imploring Joan Jones to leave the bones
Where it unfolds from there
Will tell as the story tones

So here we are in the middle
Of poems, odes, and tales
Talking about the beginning
What if the ending fails

It's not likely, my brothers
That we'll end up in the tank
We're headed for Heaven no matter the tale
For that, we have God to thank

A Gem of Value

Handsome words
Magnificent thoughts
Both part of each other
No shoulds or oughts
Truth stated simply
In elegant rhyme
A gem of value
If it be your time

In No Particular Order

John Henry
Rebel Yell
My Captain's Door
Raggedy Boy
The Magician
The Overnight Poet
Meek McCrude (Mr. Meek on Steroids)
Joan Jones
Man on a Wire
Skinny Sister
Gay Man
My Wife and I
Family Guy
My Friend the Atheist
Mr. Spiffy Doodle (and the Old Coot)
Wayne and Solomon
Penguard the Crusher
Pen (without his Guard)
Nicobod and Ichobod
John and Thomas
Me and You

Characters of note, one and all

Granddaddy's Poetry

This is not your granddaddy's poetry
This is verse of a different kind
If amused or amazed, okay
Yet these are headed for your mind
To lodge and hopefully change everything
That you ever hoped to find
Replacing it with even better
Christ within your mind

Mutual View

Kind Mind, find mine
And bring it home to You
Found sound, most profound
Flowing from You too
Sweet rhyme, all in time
To know our mutual view

Open Door

What error, what screw-up
I see no faulty place
What goodness or badness
None that inhabits our race

For we are Sons of God
We carry no fault or flaw
The only room left for error
Is when we see what the ego saw

The ego, my friends, knows nothing
Truth is beyond its grasp
It lives and perpetuates illusion
In hopes it will forever last

When we learn to truly see
With eyes of Christ, our Lord
The ego's faults will disappear
And leave open the perfect door

The World You See

I seem to like my surroundings
The world has offered me much
But lately things have changed
I've lost my taste for images and such

The world has lost its luster
Its shine has dimmed in my eyes
I no longer see its value
A greater reality it denies

You may think it is all you have
Not so great but not so bad
It gives us something to hang onto
If it were true this is all we had

Yet I'm here to give you good news
A description of a better place to be
It is nothing less than Paradise
It's the best place you'll ever see

Digital Gold

I've been digitalized, baby
I no longer have my form
Lodged on bits and internet
Trying to take it all by storm

The reach extended beyond my arm
I stretch from here to there
Making sweet words available
And bringing spring-fed fresh air

Formed up in rhyming fashion
Packaged in characters unframed
Delivered without the cover
The content is the same

Knocking at your mind for entry
Sweet ideas wrapped in gold
Tapping gently upon your door
Bearing visions of things foretold

So soak it up, my brother
Take it all back again
Absorb the sacred message
That takes away false sin

Mundane Moments

Where do we go for lunch
That is, me and my bunch
What shall we order to eat
Where shall we confirm our hunch

I know this isn't much of a conundrum
Hardly worth the time to write
Yet we spend much time in the mundane
Perhaps we should get it right

Let each moment be a blessing
Regardless of how it is spent
Live and love life fully
Soon we'll be Heaven sent
Soon we'll be Heaven sent
Soon we'll be Heaven sent

Different Roles

My mother, my brother
My father, my brother
My sister, my brother
My brother, my brother

Different strokes for different folks
Yet all the same we be
Different roles we take to wear
To cover the brothers we be

It's Like Whitman

This and that, thrown away
It's Whitman, in an inverse sort of way
None of it meaning anything
None of it was made to stay
It is a world of false illusion
It is a saddened place to stay
It is a home away from Home
Let's pack up and be on our way

Invited to Divine Repast

I'm with you Brother, I'm with you
No matter the foolish say
Just tip your hat and warn me
It will take but a moment to unstay
We'll be off and about our business
Aboard the trolley from here to there
Observing the horizon in passing
Arriving at the fabled fair
To alight and look around
To be harbored in safe Home at last
Free to live, love, and move about
To be invited to divine repast

Soon We'll Be Heaven Sent

Old Coot

Mr. Spiffy Doodle
What does the old coot say
Have you had your ear to the ground
Have you heard him wail and pray
Is he kneeling within his souldom
Is he in a position to say
That which has entered his life
And hopefully, is there to stay
Bid him look up now
Ask him to look away
From past chapters that have intrigued him
And raise his hands in a welcoming way
For God has yet to attend him
He is being bathed and groomed
Preparing to face his Creator
And leave this hopeless tomb

The Book Beneath the Cover

Brothers be brothers, my friend
No matter the skin we be in
Kin are kin, my brother
No matter the color we spin
Faces, and asses, plus appendages
All just grist for the mill
Several different flavors amaze us
And prepare us to accept The Still
For that is the book beneath the cover
For that is all that is real

Funny Guy

I farted three times in *Simple Gold*
I'm still not sure of intent
Except I work with this wise guy
Who thinks he's still unbent
He does have quite the reputation
He's likely invincible too
He dresses up well in light garments
Owns a sense of humor, often crude
But I love him with all my heart
He is brother and savior to me
I can put up with a bit of nonsense
For he means that much to me

Departure From Time

This is not a measly lot
It is a meal fit for a king
This is no tardy macaroni
It is not a meaningless fling
This is the real deal, my brother
This is what loving brings
Born and bred of each other
His Voice, holy hymnals sing
The trumpets of Heaven are pleasing
In fact they are downright sublime
Composing the gentlest of music
To amuse our departure from time

Be One

Whenever He Will Say

If it be through this door I enter
I will neither mention nor complain
I will consider myself quite blessed
My soul is no longer stained
I have been holy purified
I have seen His Holy Way
I am ready to face my Creator
Whenever He will say

One Man's Garbage

One man's garbage is another man's gold
I've heard that said for ages
Or at least that's what I've been told

I'm still unsure of its legitimacy
Nor convinced of the truth of the say
I think that what is golden
Is that which the holy repay

No coins or currency are offered
No fee for the entry exchanged
It's quite free, we've always had it
Our mind just needed rearranged

Leaving Only Roses

He knows how to turn a phrase
He knows how to split a dime
He often lends words to write
He comes round most any time

A gift is often delivered
Love and all it enshrines
A gem waiting to be taken
And shared with all who pine
For Paradise lost and forgiven
He orchestrates quite a fine line

He is the poet supreme
The One who entered my dream
Leaving only roses
To demonstrate His esteem

Penguard the Crusher

Penguard the Crusher
A man of meager means
A hollowed out stump was his throne
He longed to be king of the Norsemen
But alas, he lived all alone

Penguard the Crusher was a very large man
He stood well nigh to thirty hands
Inside he bore yet a larger heart
But life had deemed to tear it apart

His life had been filled with violence
He had savaged a man or two
His soul was chipped away with each
Yet he knew not what else to do

One day upon the path to nowhere
He encountered a tiny girl
She was lost and beaten and battered
She knew not which way to turn

In his heart, he cried for the little one
It ached as he saw her pain
She reminded him of the life he lived
Had he lived it but in vain

Pen's kingly dreams would have to wait
He had someone now to protect
This lost, lonely waif before him
The last thing he thought to expect

For much time, the waif would not speak
Her voice had lost its tone
Then one simple act of kindness
Would remind the child of home

Old Pen held out his battle-worn hand
To offer the child some bread
She had eaten not for many a day
Starvation, her impending dread

The child had been left homeless
From the battles that men do wage
She had lost both father and mother
At such a tender age

Old Pen now saw those wars he'd waged
Written upon her face
Far too much for a child to know
At such a tender age

The old Norseman's heart was broken
As he looked upon the child
Knowing the life he lived
May have cast her to the wild

He had fought and pillaged for many a year
For this was all he knew
Never a boy to be remembered
Hardness and cruelty was all his due

Penguard took mercy now on this child
He would raise her as his own
He would cease the lonely warrior's life
And make them both a home

He thought what needs the child might have
He knew so little of such
He had no gold or silver
His trove was not so much

Yet he would find a way to warm her
To ease her pain somehow
He would be the lost father to her
They would be a family now

So Pen welcomed her to his home at last
It was little for the eye to see
Yet the child smiled as she entered
She had a place to be!

The years wore on
The girl grew strong
From the love and guiding hand
Of the old and worn out Norseman
Who had long ago left his band
To raise a child abandoned
A waif who had lost her home
He now atoned for his fruitless life
He had taken this child as his own

All those years did soften Pen's heart
The girl, he truly did love
God had granted his dream somehow
A gift from Heaven above

She attended him now as he lay in bed
Life seeping from his aged frame
She had long since forgiven
The man she had never blamed

For he had given her life
And the love of a guiltless man
She now caressed his glowing face
And she let him understand
That all he had done and committed
Was washed away by love
She then gently released him
To join his Father above

You Know

You are my life, You know
Nowhere else to be
Nowhere else to go
You are my life, You know

Heaven String

String me to Heaven
Let it pull me in
I long for my forgotten Home
I yearn for the world within
My Beloved Father sits there
Among my very thoughts
At one with Him and eternity
It is what my loving brought
So much pain here
So much love there
Why wait a minute longer
To pull that string, with care

The Last Forgiveness

The last forgiveness
Is dawned upon me now
That which was buried
Deep within my heart
A sweet line of prose
Has touched me
Gently opened the hidden door
Reached inside to awaken me
To the pain I need not have borne
Let me know it was there and forgiven
Stroked my heart as it did bleed
Yet the love that quietly followed
Had eliminated my need

Behold the Hallowed Prize

Turn out the lights
There is nothing here to fear
We must be blinded first
Before we shed a tear
For the light awaits the triggering
Presuming to grace your eyes
Pull back the curtain of blindness
And behold the hallowed prize

His Holy Self

I have no thirst for water
I am the cool pool within
I have no need of leaven
I am the bread of men
Nothing leaves or wants me
I am complete within my Self
I have seen That which composed me
I am His Holy Self

We Are Brothers

Wouldn't it be just supersonic
If we all knew what we're not
And remembered just who we are
We are brothers, are we not

Pen Without His Guard

He dropped his guard
And became the pen
He loosened his ties
And let her in
This waif of his own
Whom God had sent his way
She bore the gift of life
And became of what he'd prayed
They redeemed each other
And let be The Holy Way

Traded for Diamonds Sublime

I have orphaned myself
You have orphaned yourself
Yet we are not orphans
We are of the collective Self

Oh, so little
For oh so much
A twinkling of twilight
For the universe as such

Tiny specks for giant minds
Pixels of darkness
Traded for diamonds sublime

That I Am

I am in every time
I am every place
I reside in the everyman
I live in every face
I am invisible yet present
In every kind of race
I bear no color nor breed
I am neither tall nor small
I am nothing you need feed
I am the ever present Wholeness
That grows the most sacred of seed
I am who you are
That I Am is all I be

Home

It's all a lie
Except when love appears
Tis a deception in total
The cause of all our tears

It's a blind curve at midnight
A crash and burn around every corner
It's the world as it is
Where ego makes us all mourners

It is not our home, my brother
It is not what we should see
For Home is in You, my Father
And Home is where I be

Better Off as One

Recognize our Father in each other
Know we are all the same
Let it be what it is
Lots of real estate to be reclaimed
The total includes each piece
Way better off as one
Let's all get together and party
It's time for some righteous fun

Birds to Paradise

I truly love birds
In all their varietal fame
I want to fly away with them
And learn to be untamed

The sweet swallows surrounding
The soaring eagle on high
The pelican in his droopiness
Gliding just so high
Resisting the temptation to swim it
He'll settle for low fly-bys

The brilliant cardinal flamed
The petite hummingbird's flutter
Woodpecker tapping so gently
Doves who never stutter

Beloved fellows all, I love you
You take my heart for a spin
Soon as I leave this body
We'll get together again

Every Man's Right

Once again, my Captain
You speak through familiar voice
Listening now with Christ for ears
You leave me but a simple choice

I heed now the message
Coming through loud and clear
Going on through to head quarters
Slicing right through the fear

Your words, now precious to me
I've finally seen the light
Speak to me, my Beloved
In words of everyman's right

Truth May Wait

Way beyond clever
These hallowed words do board
They come to tap your soul, my dear
They'll give you all you can afford

If they amuse you, then laugh
If they touch your heart, do cry
If they piss you off somehow
Then just let them blow on by

Yet take notice, if this be the case
There may lurk something to know
Dismiss not so lightly the matter
Truth may wait to bestow

Hold the Boat

I travel now in areas unknown
Far outside boundary or realm
Unable to fully express it
I'm captain of a wayward helm
But if this steps me to real sanity
Then hold the boat, old boy
I'm not sure I want to restrain it
It's filled with too much joy

Any Part's Good by Me

I am honored by the Home of it
Truly blessed in my part to be
Never wildly imagining
That my part would this juicy be
We must be getting nearer, Father
To uncovering the right part for me
I care not but for Your Company
Any part's good by me

Puffy the Cloud Man

Let us rest on Puffy the Cloud Man
He's lighter than a diet pie
I'll come by to join you
To play all day in the sky

A Mutual Fee

I have no intent to be
Circular, obtuse, or redundant
I defy intentional ambiguity
And stick with what I meant

I should likely stop this nonsense
I'm confusing even me
Twas nice taking a twirl with you
Let's consider it a mutual fee

Quoteth the World

The Word inside the words
Clothed as they may be
Gold inside the heart tomb
Opened for all to see
Let them fly, let them soar
Let them enter your heart
Let them live there evermore
And quoteth the world nevermore

No Sense in Being a Sensation

I'm happy to revel in obscurity
Safe and warm within my soul
No time to waste being popular
Little value in taking a poll

I pray I may help semi-secluded
Connecting with minds and souls
The body just gets in the way anyway
Of hearing what I've been told

So take my voice and message
Wrap it in words of rhyme
Hold it close to your heart, my friend
We'll know them all in good time

Round and Round

Why do you run so, sister
Trips in circles, round and round
Heading fast for nowhere
Mightn't you stand your ground
You'll never get where you're going
Letting the world take you
Round and round and round

Truest Vision

See me as Christ
Or don't see me
For we need no further lies
See me as Christ, like you
Looking with purified eyes
For all the rest are labels
Merely covering who we are
All the rest deceives us
And refuses to take us far
Ask for truest vision
It will be given as required
Open your eyes to truth
Let the illusion be retired
Open up and let God be
Ignore the truth no more
Open your eyes to Paradise
And forego the blinded whore

Rhyme in Time

I have no doubts whatsoever
Of the source of all this stuff
I have no need to be clever
In order to dress it up

The words come truly from Christ, my friend
It's time to call a spade a spade
These are gifts from Heaven
From the Well of Love they are paid

When you finally *see* them
They will burst upon your mind
In perfect sense, you will behold them
The grandest words you'll ever find

So open your heart to me
Let us play among the rhyme
Never doubt what God does hand you
It may go straight to the end of time

I'm Liking It

Not only is Your Love unconditional
It is also uncontained and unrestrained
It is the ocean filling everything
So far beyond our sight untrained

Though I see it not, I know it
It overwhelms my heart and mind
It fills me beyond comprehension
Tis the Great Revelation we find

The words, they fail me now
I can no longer use them to describe
That which has come over me
Only that I like it just fine

What the fuck?

Please Don't Send the Freaky Truck

Please don't send
The freaky truck for me
I haven't yet quite lost it
I'm still hanging around to see
What pops to the top
Of this orchid circle
What promises to set me free
Keeping both feet aside the line
We'll dabble here and there
Keep connecting as long as we need to
I don't ever remember the tear
One Mind is all we share

The Same Mind

They say I might be coming unhinged
I can only hope it is so
For to leave this world for Heaven
May require a month or so
We lose nothing in the transition
Zero is left behind
There is no loss to the Wholeness
Present all in the same Mind

Holy Essence

They are many things
Yet the same thing
Part and parcel of the whole
Prompting my heart to sing

It's so obvious
We can't even see it
That oneness is blinded by sight
And the bonds that refuse to free it

Simple yet imminently complex
The ever-part of the something
The All we all seek to be
Composed of who all we are
The holy essence of who we be

A Two Finger Poke in the Eyes

Such feeble laws
Such fragile rules
Ego unable to sustain it
This, the head of the game
The chief of all the tools
Yet you must admit, at length
That the world is pretty screwed up
It seems logical somehow
That we deserve a better leg up
One better than this lowly place
A world that often dissatisfies
A short stop between birth and death
A two finger poke in the eyes

One Kickerassaroony Poem

That was one Kickerassaroony poem
Let's bend and take another shot
No telling what will come of it
It's a small and dissimilar lot
Yet I just know, I'll like it a lot

My Main Squeeze

My funny bunny
My main squeeze-a-lot
The little woman I love
She's quite the hot-n-tot
She tickles and amazes
I'm never sure when she's not
She sure has graced my life a bunch
She is my center spot

Bobbie Brightshoes

She's the small fry of the clan
Bobbie Brightshoes with curls
A small yet gleaming star
A flag of life unfurled
The tiniest love in my life
Sweet Sasha Sue, my girl
I am forever your papa
You are forever my girl

Magical Mystery Way

It is the fabled sing about
The magical mystery tour
The Fab Four made light of it
And now there's so much more
The words paint the probables
The rhyme points the way
Listen closely and you will hear
The trumpets that sound the way
Lights pointing in the right direction
Sign posts along the way
Keep a sharp eye out, mate
Pay heed to The Holy Way

Endless Ring

My friends, the geese
Great Canadian Gray on wing
They are my heart, my love
It's quite the luminous thing
I fly with you, my brothers
Take me upon your wing
Escort me all the way to Heaven
We'll soar aloft as we sing
We'll allow the winds to carry us
Back to the endless ring

A Career Instead

Are you in it for the money
Are you in it to make amends
Are you concerned for your future
And what it has likely been
Have you wondered aloud
Why you're stuck in this place
Have you reevaluated love
And admitted its lovely face
It might be time to take a moment
And see of what will suffice
A substitute for life truly lived
A career instead of a life

A New Life as We

Let go that tenacious hold
Embrace what lies within
The world forever old
Full of decay and sin
It is quite false however
A wisp, a puff of smoke
We're trying to get your attention
So your life, you will then revoke
Trade it in for another
A better place to be
Dissolve it into nothingness
Accept a new life as We

Authentic You

A big old butt
A presumptuous gut
Jowls hanging down
With wrinkles when you frown
Best whip those bodies into shape
Or else they'll let us down

Oh, wait a minute
Hold the presses
I think they do just that
Leaving sundry little messes

It's all quite sloppy
And unappealing too
Yet yank it off, it is but cover
Hiding the authentic You

The Face of Ego

The face of ego haunts
It throws a blanket dampening
Covers up all that is truth
With a scowl, sneer, and wink

It's not such a pretty face
It was born of separate parts
It is one lonely cowboy
Surviving without a heart

An exclusionary look it gives
Wanting nothing of The Whole
Keeping a safe distance between us
To slow us in going Home

All You Need is Love

Just as the song says
All you need is love, is true
Every figure in the course of history
Has suffered from its lack
When we awake to such
And swear allegiance to love
There will be no more sorrow
We will all take its leave
The world will disappear
No one will be attacking
No one will live in fear
All to come back together
In order to be free

As Light Arrives

As light arrives
Darkness must flee
As love calls upon us
Fear must abandon thee

Let light come in
Where darkness hides
Let love reside
Where fear abides

Judging the Stakes

The judging of another
Makes us superficially wrong
We've screwed up before we started
Singing a diminished song
It is all the same reason
That we use to tear and scream
All for the same goal and purpose
We need love to close the seam
That seals us as one together
And makes us come awake
That bestows precious memory upon us
Of what has always been at stake

A Cosmic Sneer

God would never sneer
He's too far away from fear
Naught but love can leave His Face
Naught but love can linger dear
So you see, don't you
That a cosmic sneer can never be
The slightest little trace of love
Would call it to our eyes to see
The perfect face in the perfect place
Thy Holy Face

Ours to Know

May we stay in our right Mind
When ego comes a knockin
May we keep our sense of humor
Let's kick em out, let's rock em

There's a high caliber player around
Full of Mind's lovely treasures
There's a better bet to lodge
That mends the various fissures

For ego will drive a wedge
Between any two valuable thoughts
Keeping love out of the equation
And arguing for what we bought

But what we bought was bullshit
A half ass way to go
We've been deceived so far
The truth is now ours to know

Home of the Dove

All the Sons are here
Quite a gang we've caused to arrive
A small band, growing larger
With each fear that is put aside

The convergence of the Son
Is happening as we speak
I'm guessing a fair number of us
Are about to reach our peak

And on that fair mountaintop
We will plant the flag of love
Kneeling down to whisper to it
This must be the home of The Dove

A Feast of Words

The things You do with rhyme
Simply blows the mind
I feel like a kid in a candy store
Never knowing what I will find
An adventure quite grand, it is
A day spent in the Imaginerium
Amazed at the various inhabitants
And all of their happy delirium
A toy store at Christmas, in white
A feast of magnificent delight

All the Weapons

All the weapons
And all the money
That slays and slaughters
And pays and pays and pays
Can do not one iota
To make a better way

Only love, my friend, has that power
Only love can truly mend
All of the death and destruction
That haunts us from within

The battle line is drawn
Right down the middle of mind
Love and fear, the adversaries
Each hoping the truth to find

Yet fear knows not of truth
Only anger and attack, its foes
And it fights but within itself
While love waits until it goes

For fear will destroy itself
If left to its own device
Give to love, the upper hand
And our lives will truly suffice
For the instant that love does fill us
All in Heaven and Earth is right

Two Thumbs Up

Two thumbs way up
For just a simple thing
A single instance of excellence
An act of loving kindness
A sample of what salvation brings
It need not be much
This message from your heart
A unique and wondrous contribution
Of you and of That you are part

Back End Messages

A turd on the sidewalk
It keeps staring at me
If there's a message in it
I would like to quickly see
Because, you see, for some reason
My eye, it seems to offend
I'm not used to getting my messages
From some animal's backend

Jesus in a Donut

Jesus in a donut
A face we'd all like to see
But I'm afraid he's not in that donut
There's somewhere else he'll be

We believe what we want to see
We see then, what we believe
Let's stop looking for salvation in donuts
And look inside each other's belief

For Jesus, as Christ, awaits us
At the altar we refuse to see
Waiting for us to finish our donut
And see Him as we please

Due North

What better way
To battle the absurd
Than to render the outrageous
And attack it with a turd

For some times, my friend
We must decalcify the mind
And rattle those crusty cages
Of which, in ourselves, we find

Sometimes a toe stub is needed
A bump upon unseeing head
Disengage the fixed beliefs we hold
Let them come apart instead

Challenge all underlying assumptions
Give test to all beliefs
Accept no popular notions
They will give you no release

Raise your eyes to a Higher Intelligence
Accept what He puts forth
Get rid of the excess baggage
Lighten ourselves and head due north

The Stranger

He would see his brother but twice
Once as a doormat, once in a vise
The reunion was much anticipated
The time together, not so nice

The stranger would treat him badly
And then refuse to let him go
The brother was quite confused
He knew not which way to go

He viewed the bodies
All strewn upon the floor
It was obvious to him now
These men were at war

As the bodies were bagged and tagged
To him it became quite clear
That no one had forced their hand
No one had brought them here

So he cried for this stranger, this man
And his fallen comrades too
For that which had pitted them together
For that which had killed their few
And extracted its deadly due

Shutter's Island

Shutter's Island
A place of ill repute
A prison for those imprisoned
In minds that cannot refute
A point of reference
That simply does not compute
This place of insanity
This place of war
A place of much less
A place of no more
So tell me, my friends
What is the insane we see here
A place of tidy disarrangements
With a stated need for fear
A point of departure from truth
A place neither there nor here
An illusion born of insanity
And maintained by that lonely fear

What Do You See

What is it that you see in me
Am I foe or friend
Do I reside in lowly status
Or hold the key within
Is it our Lord or Satan you see
Do you value my company
Do you perceive me as free
For what you see in yourself, my brother
You must assuredly see in me

www.ingramcontent.com/pod-product-compliance
Lightning Source LLC
Chambersburg PA
CBHW071839090426
42737CB00012B/2296